Dogs to the Rescue

Dogs to the Rescue

J.C. Suarès and J. Spencer Beck

Welcome Enterprises, Inc.

New York

Compilation copyright © 1996 J.C. Suarès
Text copyright © 1996 J. Spencer Beck
Photographs copyright © individual photographers as noted
specifically on page 79, which constitutes an extension of this page

First Published in 1996 by Welcome Enterprises, Inc.
575 Broadway, New York, NY 10012

Distributed by Stewart, Tabori & Chang, Inc.,
a division of U.S. Media Holdings, Inc.
575 Broadway, New York, NY 10012

Distributed in Canada by General Publishing Company Ltd.
30 Lesmill Road, Don Mills, Ontario, Canada M3B 2T6

Distributed in Australia and New Zealand by Peribo Pty Ltd.
58 Beaumont Road, Mount Kuring-gai, NSW 2080, Australia

Distributed in all other territories by Grantham Book Services Ltd.
Isaac Newton Way, Alma Park Industrial Estate
Grantham, Lincolnshire, NG31 9SD, England

Library of Congress Card Catalog Number: 96-060746
ISBN 1-55670-508-5

Printed and bound in Italy by Arnoldo Mondadori Editore
10   9   8   7   6   5   4   3   2   1

Page 2:
ARMEN KACHATURIAN
Mozart and Captain
Kevin Butler of Engine
53/Ladder 43
New York City, 1996

Contents

More than any other members of the animal kingdom, dogs help and inspire their human companions in countless ways. My special love is for that most ancient of breeds—the Greyhound. Everyone knows them from the racetrack. What people don't know is that Greyhounds are the gentlest, sweetest dogs around. I like to call them "45-mile-per-hour couch potatoes." They may be the second fastest animal in the world, but their favorite position is on their back with their four legs up in the air. I grew up with dogs, but when I acquired my first Greyhound I discovered we were kindred spirits. Now I have six as pets, and I'm always getting new ones from the racetrack kennels. Then I do my best to find homes for them. Greyhounds are perfect "therapy dogs," and my organization tries to place our dogs with people who can most benefit from their gentle nature. They are perfect for work in nursing homes, for instance, because they won't poke too hard or jump up on people. They are perfectly content to be petted or to be able to rest their heads in a person's lap. Studies have shown that the dogs not only cheer up these senior citizens immensely, they actually lower blood pressure! My Greyhounds help people in all kinds of ways. I recently found a dog for a woman who had a serious drinking problem. This sweet dog has replaced the bottle as her best companion. Now she's up at 6 a.m. for the first time in her life, because she has to feed and walk her new pet. The two are devoted to each other. It's fitting, since, in a way, each saved the other's life. As with all breeds of our canine compatriots, these dogs are more than just man's best friends. They are often our saviors.

—Monica Bohström, member, WAG (We Adopt Greyhounds), Inc., Cheshire, Connecticut

The Dogs of Engine 53

UPI PHOTOGRAPHER
Smoky the Fire Dog
New York City, 1942

Most of the firehouses in New York City don't keep Dalmatians anymore—but we've always kept the tradition alive. In the old days, every company had one, because Dalmatians are great with horses. In Europe, Dalmatians were originally bred to accompany carriages and protect passengers from highwaymen. Firefighters here in America used them to keep other dogs from nipping at their horses' feet when they were out fighting a fire—which was really important back then. Our dog, Blaze, has it a lot easier. He prefers to sit around the firehouse. Although they are really just pets today, Dalmatians do provide a valuable service. Kids from schools visit the firehouse at least once a week, and the first thing they want to see is the Dalmatian. Luckily, Dalmatians love kids—they are real gentle—so they really help us keep the children's interest in learning about fire safety. Of course, we grown-ups love Dalmatians as much as the kids. Our captain, Kevin Butler, even has his own Dalmatian, Mozart.

Mozart loves to visit the station. It's in his genes, I guess. His father, Domino, was our company's last Dalmatian. People would come from miles around to see Domino. He was sort of a legend around here, and people really missed him after he died. That's why we keep his ashes in an urn in the firehouse. It brings us good luck.

TOM CONDON, FIREFIGHTER, ENGINE 53/LADDER 43, NEW YORK CITY FIRE DEPARTMENT

ARMEN KACHATURIAN
*Blaze with Firefighter
Tom Condon of Engine
53/Ladder 43
New York City, 1996*

Opposite:
GEORGE WOODRUFF
*Sussex Finds the Injured
Fire Fighter
n.l., 1942*

ROBIN SCHWARTZ
Bailey in Hoboken Fire Truck
Hoboken, New Jersey, 1995

Opposite:
UPI PHOTOGRAPHER
Jiggs of the Hollywood Fire
Department
Los Angeles, California, 1924

Minnie the Mutt

MARTIN HARRIS
John Robert Williams and His Boston Terrier, Peggy, at the Boy's Club Pet Show New York City, c. 1942

Every dog has his day. And for a homeless Rottweiler-spaniel mix from Hayward, California, a day that began as usual ended in an act of heroism that saved a two-year-old's life.

On a quiet Sunday stroll to church last winter, David Bruce and his wife, Pauline, noticed a friendly stray dog walking ahead of them. So did their two-year-old son, David Jr., who demanded to be let out of his stroller to pet the dog. No sooner was the energetic toddler on his feet than he dashed behind a parked car and began heading into the street. His parents watched in horror as a blue sedan sped down the road toward the parked car, which blocked the driver's view of the child. In an instant, the mutt came out of nowhere, darted right in front of David, turned, jumped up and knocked him backwards—out of the path of the car. The dog then sat down next to the child, her tongue hanging out and her tail wagging happily.

It was a miracle. And the grateful couple, who weren't able to adopt the stray because they lived in a pet-free apartment house, were heartbroken when they discovered that the local animal shelter was scheduled to put the homeless heroine to sleep. At the last minute, the Bruces told the local newspaper about the dog's act of bravery and were soon flooded with calls to adopt her.

Christened "Minnie the Mutt," the courageous canine now has a home, and is typically down-to-earth about her heroism. "Any mutt would have done the same thing," she tells one and all.

ED.

E. W. Weinberger,
U.S. Air Force
*Sgt. Francis M. Dowdy and
Paratrooper Joe of the 10th
Rescue Unit Prepare to Jump
from a Douglas C-47
Ladd Air Force Base,
Alaska, c. 1948*

Opposite:
Photographer unknown
*Rescue Husky Parachuting
to Scene
Canada, 1948*

Bred in the Bone

My dog Sophie is three-quarters German Shepherd and one-quarter gray wolf, so she's partly wild. Her father, Sam, was a working police dog in Arizona, bred for search and rescue. But Sophie is just a pet, trying to lead a quiet life in the big city.

I had a late gig one evening, and decided to take Sophie to the playground before it. Even late, there were usually a lot of dog owners with their pets there, but that night when I got there the playground was empty. I couldn't disappoint the excited Sophie, so I started tossing a ball for her as I always do. I didn't notice the rough-looking guy behind me until he was about to grab me—and even though he was moving slowly (I think he was pretty strung out), it was pretty scary.

As I darted away from him, Sophie came galloping back with the ball in her mouth, tail wagging. Instinctively I yelled, "Sophie, help!" Suddenly she dropped her ball and an entirely different look came to her face. Her hackles were up and her teeth bared. I'd never seen anything like it before. Then she started for the guy. Stupidly, now that I think about it, he stood his ground. He started fumbling in his pocket. Who knows what he was trying to get out, since a split second later Sophie rushed him, knocked him down, and got him by the collar. She stood on top of him as his free arm flailed and his legs kicked, trying to get her off. He even got her a couple of times with his boots, but she wouldn't budge.

He must have realized he couldn't fight her off, because he started pleading with me. "Your dog's crazy!" he kept saying.

Normally, Sophie avoids conflicts as much as possible—the wolf in her hates close crowds and noise. And the dog in her loves to play so much I have a hard time getting her to drop the ball. Now here she was, locked with this would-be mugger in a full embrace. And it took me a while to get her off. Wolf blood or not, she showed me that she has as much drive as her dad. I guess bravery is bred in the bone after all.

JANA MARTIN, PERFORMER, NEW YORK CITY

MARY BLOOM
Partners
New York City, 1984

The Wives of Beep-Beep

PHOTOGRAPHER UNKNOWN
*Pete the Pup Nursing a Goat
Hollywood, c. 1930*

When I moved to New York, the first dog I got was Lulu—a Yorkshire Terrier puppy. Later, I got another Yorkie named Beep-Beep. Lulu made it quite clear from the beginning that she didn't like poor Beep-Beep. In fact, she hated Beep-Beep, and for a long time Beep-Beep just worshipped Lulu. They were like a married couple—a married couple in an arranged marriage. I mean, Cupid had shot his arrow into Beep-Beep, but Cupid had not shot his arrow into Lulu. But the years went on and they had a certain relationship. Finally, at age eleven, Lulu died. After her death, Beep-Beep just lost it. He stopped eating and got weaker and weaker. I didn't think he would live much longer. Eventually, I decided to get a new puppy. I brought home Minky, a

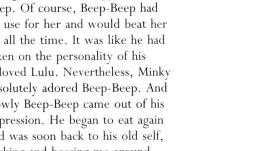

Chinese Crested, and she was very young and just worshipped Beep-Beep. Of course, Beep-Beep had no use for her and would beat her up all the time. It was like he had taken on the personality of his beloved Lulu. Nevertheless, Minky absolutely adored Beep-Beep. And slowly Beep-Beep came out of his depression. He began to eat again and was soon back to his old self, barking and bossing me around. Then I got another Chinese Crested puppy, Lily, and she worshipped Beep-Beep, too. So even though Beep-Beep never loved both of them like he loved Lulu, he grew old having two young wives who really saved his life. Now he's fourteen years old and his wives are three—and he looks like he's going to keep going for a long time.

TAMA JANOWITZ, DOG LOVER AND AUTHOR, *SLAVES OF NEW YORK* AND *BY THE SHORES OF GITCHI GUMEE*

UPI Photographer
*Gunnar Kasson and Balto
at the Unveiling of Balto's
Statue in Central Park
New York City, 1925*

Opposite:
UPI Photographer
*Gunnar Kasson and His
Dog, Balto, Leader of the
Sled Team that Brought
Medicine to Diptheria-
Stricken Nome, Alaska
n.l., 1925*

Overleaf:
Reuters Photographer
*Lining Up before Minstrel the
Cat at the Metropolitan
Police Dog Training School
Keston, England, 1987*

Boo, Lifesaver

KENT AND DONNA
DANNEN
*Ch. Karibou in the
Nursing Home
Boulder, Colorado, 1989*

In 1989 the British national charity PRO Dogs, based in Kent, England, gave a medal to a dog called Boo for drawing attention to a cancerous mole on the leg of her owner, Mrs. Bonita Whitfield, which enabled her to get life-saving treatment. Each year PRO Dogs gives three awards to dogs, for Life Saving, Devotion to Duty, and Pet of the Year. The nomination for this dog was picked up following a letter in *The Lancet* by Doctor Hywel Williams and Mr. Andrew Pembroke of Kings College Hospital, London. Understandably, there is growing concern about the increasing incidence of melanoma (skin cancers), and the little Whippet-type dog called Boo continually drew attention to the mole on the back of Bonita's leg, by sniffing at it. Although the owner did not appreciate this attention and tried to shoo the dog away, Boo was so insistent that at last Bonita went to her doctor. She was immediately referred to Kings College Hospital where the mole was removed and confirmed as cancerous. Dr. Williams put forward the theory that such cancers may emit a distinctive odor which the very sensitive scenting ability of the dog may be able to pick up.

With so many more people suffering from skin cancers today, it is important for people to be aware that if their dog is interested in a mole growing on any part of their body, it is worth immediate attention and a visit to the doctor!

LESLEY SCOTT-ORDISH, EDITOR, *ARGOS* MAGAZINE; FOUNDER, PRO DOGS AND PETS AS THERAPY, AND VICE PRESIDENT, HEARING DOGS FOR THE DEAF AND COMPANION ANIMALS FOR INDEPENDENCE

Overleaf:
KENT AND DONNA
DANNEN
*Samoyed Hearing Ear Dog
Estes Park, Colorado, 1989*

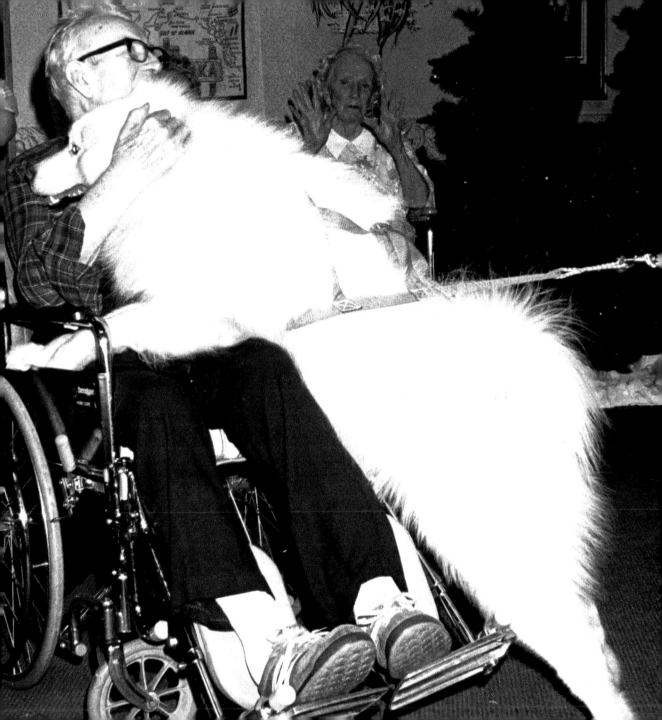

My Hero

LIZZIE HIMMEL
The Kiss
New York City, 1991

My dog was always my hero. I remember him licking away my tears when I was sad.

MAN, OF HIS CHILDHOOD PET

Good Influence

PHOTOGRAPHER UNKNOWN
Roddy McDowall in
Lassie Come Home
Hollywood, California, 1942

In a paper entitled "The Influence of Dogs on the Behavior of Juveniles in the Big Cities," Professor R. Bergler and Christa Westendorf of Germany studied the influence of pet dogs on 480 children, ages fourteen to eighteen. The results showed that children with dogs were more content with their lives, more goal-oriented at school and work, and had positive relationships with superiors. Children who did not have dogs had more alcohol and tobacco use, conflicts with parents, and self-doubt.

ED.

Hunter's Run

Most people don't think of Beagles as being terribly heroic. There's Snoopy, of course—who's heroic in his way! But Beagles are mostly cute and crazy—great companions but hardly heroic. My dog Hunter was an exception. Like most Beagles, he was a bit skittish and he bayed at anything that moved, especially at night. But we loved him, and it broke our hearts that we had to give him away when we moved to the city. In any case, Hunter wouldn't have liked the city—not enough rabbits to bark at. And he loved to bark! After a long and hard search, we found a perfect home for him—a Beagle breeder where Hunter would have lots of friends to play with.

Hunter's new master was a bit exasperated at first by Hunter's insomnia and decidedly noisy personality. So she decided to give him to her husband, who drove a truck part-time to bring in some extra money. The husband had had a few near misses on the road lately after dozing off, and his wife had been begging him to give up his late-night runs altogether. Hunter saved the day. He had always liked to take long rides. The trucker outfitted the cabin of the truck with an elaborate nest for Hunter to sleep in during the day, so he was happy to sit up all night. And his constant baying at night kept his new owner awake on even the dullest stretches of road. In fact, Hunter eventually began to bark at the first sign that his new owner was falling asleep. Not only did Hunter save his new owner's livelihood, he probably saved his life as well.

James Scott, social worker, San Francisco

Photographer unknown
Howling for Mary Miles Minter and Director Henry King
Los Angeles, California
c. 1920

Overleaf:
Photographer unknown
Rex, King of the Wild Horses, and Rin-Tin-Tin Jr., in The Law of the Wild
n.l., c. 1930's

The Bomb Squad

Our unit may be smaller than the other canine-enforcement units at Miami International Airport, but our dogs are in the business of thwarting terrorists—and that's a pretty big job in my book. And our dogs have to be really smart. That's why we use mostly Labradors and German Shepherds—and even Poodles, which many people don't realize are among the very brightest dogs. Our dogs and their handlers are trained to find explosives, but how they actually do so has to remain a secret, for obvious reasons. Of course, all these dogs have finely honed noses. It's not an easy job. The dogs and their handlers have to spend three months training at Lackland Air Force Base in Texas —it's a pretty rigorous course. Then we continue to train them three to five days a week here at the airport. We have a "Bomb Search Building" set up for just that purpose. Because it's such a serious task to sniff out a bomb, our dogs are never cross-trained with narcotics dogs or the dogs used for detecting illegal plant and animal matter. We don't want them to find anything but explosives—and luckily they never do! Besides sterilizing areas for presidential visits or visits by heads of state, we keep the airport safe for the average traveler. That's the most important thing. It's a great team effort.

SGT. JOSEPH RESCHETAR, CANINE EXPLOSIVE ORDNANCE DETECTION (EOD), METRO-DADE POLICE DEPARTMENT, MIAMI

UPI PHOTOGRAPHER
Lancer, Marijuana-sniffing
German Shepherd Dog,
and Handler Jack Grinham,
State Trooper
Logan International Airport,
Boston, 1973

Overleaf:
PHOTOGRAPHER UNKNOWN
Rin-Tin-Tin in
Dog of the Regiment
Los Angeles, California, 1927

Angels of Mercy

One of the largest searches for a missing person in recent memory took place in one of the smallest communities in America. Galena Hollow, Missouri, a tiny hamlet in the middle of the Ozarks, became the focus of national attention for three long days in March of 1996 with the disappearance of Joshua Carlisle Coffey, a ten-year-old with Down's syndrome who had wandered away from his home late one afternoon.

After having been lost for seventy-two hours in freezing temperatures and rough terrain, the youngster was presumed by many to be dead. But the parents of the child and the tenacious local sheriff's department —not to mention 350 volunteers from six states—never gave up hope. And neither did two stray dogs. Later nicknamed "Baby" and "Angel," a homeless brown Dachs-hund-Beagle mix and his companion, a mixed-breed Blue Heeler, led searchers to the boy after the sheriff department's team of rescue dogs had finally closed in on an area where they believed the child would be found. Reclining face-down in a gully about a mile and a quarter north of his home, little Josh had been kept alive by the two strays, who had slept on top of the child to keep him warm and even fetched food for him from the provisions of local rescue workers. Quickly dubbed "Missouri's Little Miracle," Joshua Coffey had suffered from over-exposure but otherwise was in amazingly good shape.

As for the miracle mutts themselves, they finally found a home with the relieved and grateful Coffey family. "The angels just slipped in beside Josh," Mrs. Coffey said. "Those dogs had wings for sure."

ED.

KENT AND DONNA DANNEN
Tundra, Samoyed, on Caribou Pass Arapaho National Forest, Colorado, 1981

Demining Dogs

ANTONÍN MALÝ
Kazan, U.S.S.R., 1988

While negotiators from around the world continue the frustrating scramble to keep some sort of peace in war-torn Bosnia, heroic teams of specially trained dogs from the United States are actually saving lives.

In tiny Bosnia an estimated two to six million land mines strewn throughout the countryside are responsible for the daily deaths of soldiers and civilians alike. Faced with the daunting task of cleaning up this dangerous mess, the U.S. Army and Department of Defense have begun training teams of highly intelligent dogs—Shepherds, Terriers, and mixed breeds—who will comb the Bosnian countryside hunting for a most deadly prey. Among the first dogs sent overseas were Rega and Chita, two crack deminers trained by the Texas-based Global Training Academy, the world's premier source of demining dogs. Trained to locate explosives by scent, these dogs receive at least twenty weeks of highly sensitive training, twelve weeks longer than that for other types of "bomb dogs." Although a trained deminer working four to six hours a day can clear only a 200-square-meter area (the dogs locate the bombs, which are then detonated by army personnel), some twenty demining teams have finally begun to clean up a sizable portion of Bosnia's deadly landscape. As the peacekeepers bicker at the bargaining table, our canine comrades-in-arms have already distinguished themselves on the frontline.

ED.

U.S. Army Signal Corps
Photographer
War Dog
n.l., c. 1944

Opposite:
Photographer unknown
Kaiser, German Messenger
Dog Captured behind
British Lines
France, c. 1942

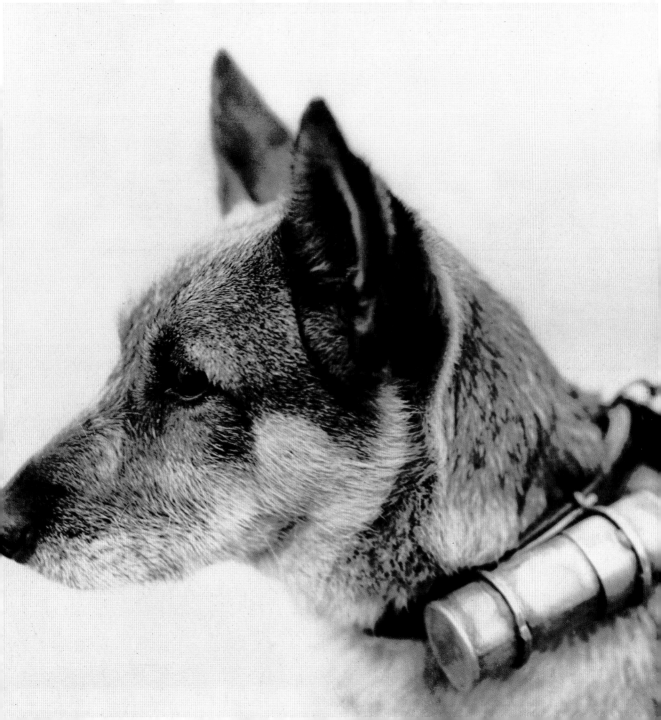

IRVING HABERMAN
Beach Patrol
U.S. Coast Guard
n.l., c. 1943

The Snake Terriers

JOHN DRYSDALE
Bush Baby (Marmoset)
Getting a Ride on a Black
Labrador,
London, 1990

The U.S. Department of Agriculture has a very special problem on Guam—snakes. And we have a very special group of dogs to deal with it. Our dogs are mostly Jack Russell Terriers and Fox Terrier mixes, which were originally bred to hunt varmint like rats and moles. But our team has been trained to hunt snakes. And no one hates snakes more than my dogs. This is a fairly new operation, but the problem really began after World War II, when a seemingly benign serpent called a "Brown Tree Snake" was introduced to Guam via military cargo from other islands in the South Pacific. Unfortunately, the snakes had no natural predators on the island. Once biologists noticed that some eight of the island's dozen or so bird species had suddenly become extinct, the USDA began to act. My main job right now is containment. Most planes that leave Guam stop off in Hawaii. If these snakes ever got onto Hawaii, it would be an ecological disaster. Not to mention the mainland. And the snakes are tricky. We've even found them in the wheel compartments of airplanes!

I train my dogs in San Francisco, and then we transport them to Guam. Nothing leaves the island without our dogs doing a thorough search first. And these terriers are tenacious—if there's a snake coiled up somewhere they'll find it. These dogs might not seem heroic to some people, but once one species is extinct, others are sure to follow. And that ultimately means Man, too.

MEL ROBLES, CANINE COORDINATOR-TRAINER, USDA, WESTERN REGION

Shy Katy

Search-and-rescue dogs are trained to be heroic. But my shy Australian Shepherd named Katy seemed like an unlikely candidate for such an honor. I hadn't properly "socialized" her as a puppy and she has always been terrified of other dogs and people—not a great quality for rescue work. But I knew the bond between a handler and his dog is the most important thing, and Katy was devoted to me. Still, I had my doubts.

The first test came when Katy was three years old and we were called to assist a rescue effort at a large trailer park that had been devastated by a tornado. My doubts were confirmed when we arrived at the gruesome scene and Katy immediately began to tremble. The swarms of rescue workers and the incredible commotion were just too much for her. I was reluctant to begin the search. Then I put Katy's orange reflective collar on, as I had always done during our training sessions, and she immediately stopped shaking. She looked at me enthusiastically, as if to say, "Now I'm ready to work!" She was truly heroic over the next three days, so undaunted, in fact, that the rescue team used her specifically to crawl into small spaces they had dug out looking for survivors. Today Katy is still terribly shy, but she does a Superman-like transformation the minute I put her collar on. Recently, she saved an elderly gentleman suffering from Alzheimer's disease who had wandered away from his house as a storm was approaching. Searchers on foot had given up, but Katy found her man. And in the nick of time. Had he been caught in the storm, he surely would have died.

DANA KAMMERLOHR, CANINE OFFICER, BARRY COUNTY [MISSOURI] SHERIFF'S DEPARTMENT, AND VOLUNTEER, MISSOURI SEARCH AND RESCUE CANINE

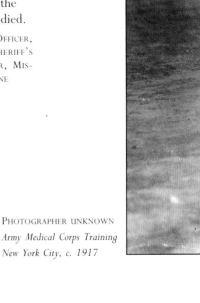

PHOTOGRAPHER UNKNOWN
Army Medical Corps Training
New York City, c. 1917

PHOGRAPHER UNKNOWN
Robert Peary and his Dogs on the Roosevelt
n.l., 1909

Opposite:
PHOGRAPHER UNKNOWN
The Dogs of Roald Amundsen's South Pole Expedition at Rest
South Pole, 1911

All in a Day's Work

The Oklahoma bomb blast stunned the world, leaving destruction, grief and trauma in its wake. Not all the wounds were physical, however, and where a different kind of healing was needed, Partner's work began.

He appears to be an unassuming, middle-aged dog—just your average Golden Retriever. But there's nothing average about Partner, who, with his Delta Society/Pet Partners teammates, Kris and Amanda Butler, won Delta Society's 1995 "Family Service Award" for therapy animals. Together, the three assist health-care professionals at Southwest Medical Center's Jim Thorpe Rehabilitation Hospital in Oklahoma City, working with therapists and their clients in physical therapy, speech therapy, memory, sequencing, and motivation. For Partner, it's all in a day's work. And when a terrorist bomb left Oklahoma City in turmoil, it wasn't only blast survivors who were scarred. Rescuers, counselors, and health-care providers were almost as traumatized as those they sought to help. Partner's extraordinary aptitude for his work, and his unconditional love, made him a preferred treatment for these professionals. And his patient understanding began the healing process in those he served. According to Kris Butler, Partner's most measurable impact has been on his human family. "He helps us to shine," she says, "to help others and feel so good about ourselves. . . . It has been said that animals open doors so that healing can begin. Let us humans always listen so we hear opportunity when it knocks on those doors . . . and creatively work with our animals to open them."

DELTA SOCIETY

KENT AND DONNA DANNEN
Patrick Dannen and Golden Retriever Puppy in Training to be an Assistance Dog
Longmont, Colorado, 1995

Overleaf:
UPI PHOTOGRAPHER
Dalmation War Dog Jumps Barbed Wire
n.l. c. 1944

Dugan's Race

RON KIMBALL
The Leaders
Chester, California, 1995

The Iditarod is the biggest sled-dog event in the world. It is also the most dangerous. A grueling 1,049-mile trek across the mountains and frozen tundra of Alaska, the marathon event takes anywhere from nine days to a couple of weeks to complete. And not everybody—or every dog—finishes the race. One athlete who has is Libby Riddles. A sixteen-year veteran of the sport and the author of *Race Across Alaska*, she had the honor in 1985 of being the first woman ever to win the competition. Today she admits she was lucky to finish the race—much less win it. "My lead dog that year was Dugan, an exceptional Alaskan husky I had raised myself. His good genes and training really came in handy towards the end of the race when a blinding Arctic ground storm threatened to delay the event by days. I had just reached a checkpoint and had the option of waiting the storm out or continuing on. I decided to go for it." It was a risky move. "There are markers along the trail—about three to a mile—and at one point neither the dogs nor I could see them anymore. I had to leave my dogs to find them first and then go back to them and mush them on. Many dogs would have turned back had their musher walked ahead without them—but not Dugan! He knew how much this meant to me. Had he run off, I might have died. Taking on the storm that year was pretty gutsy, I guess, and it won me the race. But it was my incredible team of dogs—especially Dugan—who saved the day . . . and me!"

ED.

Overleaf:
PER WICHMANN
Winter Race
Sweden, 1995

Saving Duke

On my tenth birthday I was presented with Duke, a six-week-old, bright-eyed, and big-pawed pup. What a beauty! Duke was part–German Shepherd, part–Alaskan husky with handsome black and tan markings. Everywhere we went people commented on what a good looking dog he was. We were inseparable. That Christmas I got a new hockey stick. Never mind that I didn't have a pair of skates or the foggiest notion of how to play the game—I had Duke as a teammate and some giant Sweethearts candy for pucks. What else did I need? We set out on a cold, late December day to find some ice. Behind the county fairgrounds were some deserted irrigation ponds that were frozen over—perfect for playing boy vs. dog hockey. Just as I was about to run onto the ice, Duke began barking at me. Not to be outdone, I yelled back and kept running closer to the center of the pond. I'm not quite sure exactly what happened next. I remember seeing Duke airborne in what seemed to be a ten-foot-high leap, arcing through the air and then landing, crashing through the ice. The next thing I saw was Duke's cold and wet face looking up at me from the frigid water. Crying hysterically, I tried to hand him my hockey stick, afraid he would drown. Duke couldn't swim—he had never been taught! He had never even been in the water before. But by some miracle he didn't drown. He could swim! Not only that, he instinctively and bravely saved me from falling through the ice. Duke died tragically about a year later, and even as an adult I miss him. However, his courage and self-sacrificing loyalty lives on every day in my memory and in my heart.

JOHN CURTIS-MICHAEL,
ENTERTAINER, NEW YORK CITY

UPI PHOTOGRAPHER
Fixing a Barrel to a St. Bernard's Collar
St. Bernard Hospice, Switzerland, 1927

ABEL & CO.
On Top of Mr. Antonio
Washington, DC, c. 1922

Opposite:
ROBIN SCHWARTZ
Jake and Mugs
Ohio, 1990

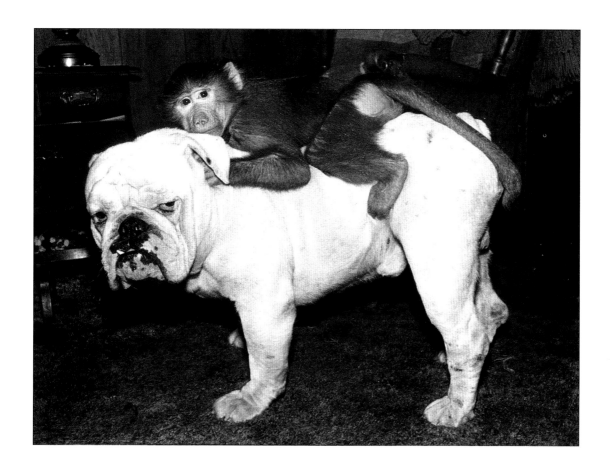

My Eyes, My Hands

MARY BLOOM
New Eyes
New York City, 1982

Guide dogs have been serving people who are blind for over eighty years now. In the past, these dogs were typically German Shepherds. Today, many different breeds of dogs assist people with a wide array of other disabilities. And the results have been astounding. At the Delta Society, a national group with headquarters in Renton, Washington, awareness of the health benefits to humans these animals provide is the organization's top priority.

Susan Duncan, a registered nurse who is the Coordinator of the National Service Dog Center for the Delta Society, has first-hand knowledge of her field. She has been living with multiple sclerosis for eighteen years. For a decade she managed as best she could with a disease that was progressively worsening. Joe, a part–German Shepherd, part–Great Dane stray whom Susan saved from euthanasia, came to the rescue. Trained by Susan herself, Joe helps his mistress with the daily tasks most people take for granted—like getting out of bed in the morning: "Joe pulls my feet off of the edge of the bed and then uses his head to swing me up to a sitting position." Incredibly, Joe also helps with the banking ("I punch in the code at my ATM, he grabs the money") and shopping ("Joe can reach things I can't and carries it all in a backpack on his back").

No longer dependent on others to help her manage her day-to-day life, Susan is now free to pursue activities she couldn't possibly sustain previously. "I had always loved gardening. Now I've trained Joe to dig flower beds for me. He loves to do it. And my garden is finally thriving." Thanks to Joe the service dog, so is Susan.

ED.

WIDE WORLD
PHOTOGRAPHER
Butch Guards an RAF
Twin-Gunner
Western Desert, Libya, c.1942

Opposite:
U.S. COAST GUARD
Soogie, Morale Builder
First Class and Veteran of
Sicily, Salerno, and
Normandy Invasions
France, 1944

Overleaf:
ROBIN SCHWARTZ
Pete, Hoboken K-9
Hoboken, New Jersey, 1993

Pet Partners

MARY BLOOM
James and Suzanne
New York City, 1984

If a handsome English Setter named Hambleton is denied a chance to crawl into bed and snuggle with his young friends at the National Cancer Institute of the National Institutes of Health, in Bethesda, Maryland, he actually pouts. "Hambone" doesn't care that some of his young patients have AIDS. For him, that disease poses no threat and his greatest pleasure is snuggling up to a young, bed-bound patient and taking a leisurely nap. To these patients, he brings a sense of love and acceptance often not conveyed by human visitors.

This remarkable animal, along with his sibling, Gandalf, and their "parents," Shari and Wayne Sternberger, form a Delta Society/Pet Partners team that is much in demand, with a "resume" that fills pages. It is no wonder they won Delta Society's 1995 "Service to an Institution Award" for therapy animals.

Gandalf and Hambleton are particularly known for their "bed visits," with Hambleton, in particular, loving to snuggle up against the client. Both dogs have an uncanny ability to identify each person's greatest need at that moment, lying quietly to absorb tears or curling up with a restless child to share a pillow and a snore. Hambleton's first visit to a young AIDS patient named Heather amazed doctors and nurses, who saw this frustrated and hyperactive child become entirely focused on the animal, stroking his fur, counting his toes, and giving him the biggest possible hugs while his tail flapped in high gear. By the next visit, Heather had passed away. But at her memorial, which included photographs of those who'd mattered most, one photograph took center stage: Hambleton and Heather, snuggled in bed, together.

DELTA SOCIETY

UPI Photographer
Comforted at the Beachhead
France, 1944

Opposite:
U.S. Marine Corps
Photographer
Butch Guards over Private
Rez Hester's Nap
Iwo Jima, 1945

Acknowledgements

The author wishes to thank the following
organizations for their kind help in compiling this book:
Delta Society, 289 Perimeter Road East, Renton, WA 98055
PRO Dogs National Charity and Pets as Therapy, 4–6 New Road,
Ditton, Kent ME20 6AD England
WAG (We Adopt Greyhounds), Inc., PO Box 519,
Cheshire, Connecticut, 06410, (203) 655-7317

Pages 56, 74:
Reprinted from InterActions (Vol. 13, No. 4, 1995)
with permission of Delta Society.

Photo Credits

Indicia

Designed and edited by J.C. Suarès
Text compiled by J. Spencer Beck
Text edited by Jane Martin
Design Assistance by Christy Trotter
Drawings by J.C. Suarès